TURNING GREAT IDEAS INTO GREAT COMPANIES

4 Steps
Let's Keep It Simple

Bill Bierds and David Dunne
With Michael Ransom

www.tgigc.io

Copyright © 2020 by WCC LLC
All rights reserved

"What you get by achieving your goals is not as important as what you become by achieving your goals"

Henry David Thoreau

Table of Contents

INTRODUCTION

CHAPTER 1

THE CONCENTRIC GROWTH MODEL

CHAPTER 2

SELF-ASSESSMENT

   PRODUCT SELF-ASSESSMENT

   SALES SELF-ASSESSMENT

   CUSTOMER SELF-ASSESSMENT

   MARKETING SELF-ASSESSMENT

CHAPTER 3

THE PRODUCT QUADRANT

   YOUR SOLUTION

   MARKET RELEVANCE AND TIMING

   COMPETITION

   PRODUCT EVOLUTION

   QUALITY CONTROL

   DELIVERY SERVICES

   LEGAL PROTECTION

   SCALABILITY

   CUSTOMER SATISFACTION

CHAPTER 4

THE SALES QUADRANT

   HIRING, TRAINING, AND RECRUITING SALESPEOPLE

1. RECRUITING
2. INTERVIEWING
3. EXTENDING THE OFFER
4. DEVELOPTING A PRODUCTIVE EMPLOYEE
5. DEVELOPING AN ONBOARDING PROGRAM
6. RETAINING GOOD SALESPEOPLE

SALES ACCOUNT PLANS

   TYPES OF ACCOUNT PLANS

   ENSURING THAT ACCOUNT PLANNING WORKS

SALES CYCLE

CLOSING DEALS

SALES PIPELINE MANAGEMENT

CHAPTER 5

THE CUSTOMER QUADRANT

   CUSTOMER EXPERIENCE

   CUSTOMER SERVICE

   CUSTOMER CARE

   REFERENCES AND ADVOCATES

   CUSTOMER FEEDBACK

   THE CUSTOMER IS ALWAYS RIGHT

CHAPTER 6

THE MARKETING QUANDRANT

   YOUR BRAND

   YOUR STORY

   TYPES OF MARKETING

    WEBSITES

    SOCIAL MEDIA

    BUSINESS NETWORKING

    ADVERTISING

    PUBLIC RELATIONS

    EVENTS

    TRADE SHOWS

    INFLUENCERS

    STRATEGIC PARTNERSHIP

  RETURN ON INVESTMENT: IS YOUR MARKETING EFFECTIVE?

  THE PIECES FALL INTO PLACE

CHAPTER 7

STAY THE COURSE

Appendix

  PRODUCT SELF-ASSESSMENT

  SALES SELF-ASSESSMENT

  CUSTOMER SELF-ASSESSMENT

  MARKETING SELF-ASSESSMENT

Recommended Reading

Acknowledgements

About the Authors

INTRODUCTION

*"Genius is making complex ideas simple,
not making simple ideas complex"*
Albert Einstein

So, let's keep it simple! *Turning Great Ideas into Great Companies* is an easy-to-read 4 step guide for business owners and business leaders of any size in any industry. It is intended to help raise awareness and help the reader understand the four components critical to success: Product, Sales, Customer, and Marketing.

Who should read this book:

- Budding entrepreneurs. This book is a great first step. Whether you have been dreaming for 50 years or 50 seconds, this book is designed to develop your business around your great idea.
- Established business owners and leaders who are feeling the exhilaration and/or anxiety that comes with accelerated growth. This book will help you break through to the next plateau. And for businesses that may have stalled or are listing in heavy seas, this book can help you right the ship.
- Anyone looking to tap into some entrepreneurial spirit. We all have it. If you have not yet identified that great

idea, pick up this book anyway. Regardless of what you do personally or professionally, we are all looking for fresh ideas to achieve success, and frankly, to not waste any more time. It is not enough to simply be passionate about something you are doing. You need to build a foundation for success. This short book with 4 simple steps will help guide your way.

Small and medium size businesses are the engine of every economy in every country in the world. In the United States, the U.S. Small Business Association reported that greater than 40% of the Gross National Product (GDP) comes from small businesses. Globally, the World Trade Organization reports that small businesses represent nearly 55% of the GDP in developed economies. These statistics clearly demonstrate that small businesses are not just a big part of our economy, they are our economy. When GDP grows jobs are available, wages are higher, living standards are better and poverty goes down. One could argue we each have a civic duty and we all should be *Turning Great Ideas into Great Companies*.

Bill Bierds and David Dunne know that transforming ideas into successful ventures is not easy. Bill is information technology veteran and has had the entrepreneurial flame burning throughout his career at companies like Citigroup, IBM, and his latest venture at, BCC Group. These companies have provided him with multiple opportunities to experience and overcome the challenges associated with great ideas and what makes them succeed.

David Dunne has led many business transformations, mergers, and acquisitions centered around technology. His experience ranges from serving as a Chief Data and Analytics Officer, to venture capitalism. His entrepreneurial experiences have given him a clear understanding of the key metrics and data that a business must have to thrive.

Bill and David have written this book to share what they have learned. Their goal is to help you succeed. Their straight-forward advice is to invest uniformly in, and never take your eye off four strategic business pillars: product, sales, customer, and marketing. Although it may seem practical or more fun to concentrate on the progress of one pillar at a time, strategically the focus must be on all four. A shift toward one at the expense of the others can trigger disaster; companies that concentrate on and consistently develop the four pillars are more likely to succeed than those that don't. Bill and David call their model the Concentric Growth Model (CGM). No matter where you are in your business's evolution, their advice will apply because the core needs of a business can be synthesized into these critical key points. This book helps explain these needs in a way that can be quickly grasped and tailored to make a lasting difference to your business.

The seeds for this book were planted in the early 2000s, when many dot-com businesses, that had flourished in prior years, were going out of business at an accelerated pace. Online retail companies such as eToys.com, GeoCities, Go.com, Pets.com, Webvan, and Boo.com struggled and many failed. The authors noticed that these companies focused on the pizzazz of their ideas rather than <u>concentric growth</u> as they were going from internet darlings to internet disasters.

The authors acknowledge that there are many key elements to running a successful business—tremendous financial rigor, for example—that are not included in this book. Rather than repeat information covered well in other publications, Bill and David have chosen to keep it simple. There are plenty of books with thousands of pages written about four areas of focus in this book. Start by reading and/or listening to this book. Then take the self-assessment that can be found in the appendix of the book or online at tgigc.wordpress.com. Use this new knowledge to determine what you need and keep studying. We have provided some book ideas for you in the final pages as well.

This book is intended to help passionate, hard-working people with great ideas develop and maintain success. All the best to you on this amazing journey!

CHAPTER 1

THE CONCENTRIC GROWTH MODEL

"Achieving success is like hitting a moving target. Both require accuracy, the ability to counteract external factors, and adjusting the sight when necessary."
Valerie J. Lewis Coleman

The Concentric Growth Model (CGM) is a template. It is based on the premise that orchestrated growth must be iterative and focused. This is the best way to build business value over time. The primary areas for this growth are product, sales, customer, and marketing (Figure 1-1 & 1-2). With a consistent focus on maturing in these four areas, you will significantly increase your company's chances for sustained growth and prosperity.

Each quadrant shown in Figure 1-2 is made up of several major components that you should assess repeatedly to determine your business's health. Each one will be explained (with examples) in Chapters 2 through 6.

The CGM is of value to you because you can use it to assess your business's health in key areas, focus on high-priority situations, and develop action plans to address conditions that need attention. The following chapters will help you think through that assessment.

Figure 1-1. The four quadrants of the Concentric Growth Model

Sales

- Hiring, Training, and retaining salespeople
- Targets, opportunities, and duds
- Sales account plans
- Sales cycle
- Deal Closure

Customer

- Customer life cycle
- Customer experience
- Customer service
- Customer care
- References and advocates
- Customer Feedback

Product

- Relevance and timing
- Competition
- Product evolution
- Quality control
- Legal
- Scalability
- Customer satisfaction

Marketing

- Brand and story
- Websites
- Social Media
- Business networking
- Advertising and public relationship
- Events and trade shows
- Influencers and analysts
- Strategic Partnerships

Figure 1-2. Quadrant components

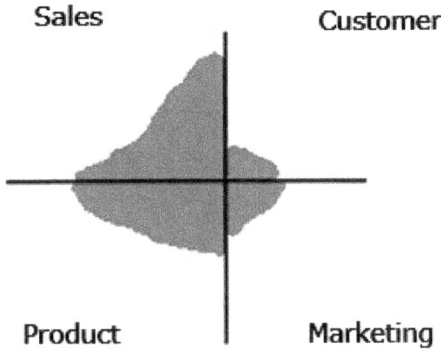

Figure 1-3. Inequitable or partial growth

Figure 1-3 illustrates one permutation of what inequitable or uneven growth would look like using the model. This is typical of a company that starts with a great idea
(product). They pour their hearts and souls into the product and the sales and neglect the customer and marketing. Yes, this company has indeed seen success in building a quality product and it has also managed to grow sales and build revenue, but because the customer and marketing quadrants have been virtually ignored, they have taken a very short-term view of their place in the market. Although initially the revenue stream seems strong, in the long run the lack of focus on servicing their customers and marketing their idea will limit the sustainability of their venture. The ultimate downside of this situation is the company will slowly start to

falter. And if they should manage to survive, their ability to raise capital to grow and expand will be severely hampered.

Figure 1-4 illustrates a business that has developed all four quadrants in concert. It is important to establish this growth pattern early in the business's life cycle, for it lays a foundation for controlled growth as the sales revenue and customer results grow. While nothing guarantees success, this is sure a great start! The main point is that all quadrants must be developed for the company to grow and maximize the value proposition.

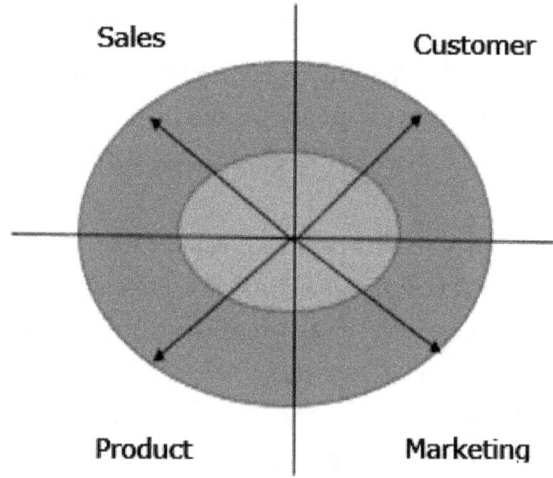

Figure 1-4 Concentric Growth Model

CHAPTER 2

SELF-ASSESSMENT

"You need to leave the city of your comfort and go into the wilderness of your intuition. What you'll discover will be wonderful. What you'll discover is yourself."
Alan Alda

This chapter contains self-assessment questions to help you understand how well you are positioned for growth in the product, sales, customer, and marketing quadrants. The assessment is fast and nonscientific; the results rely on your integrity and gut check on the reality of where you are positioned in each dimension. Rate (check) each question from 1 to 3. Use the following as your guide:

- 1. You have given this a lot of thought and you have executed
- 2. You are aware, and you have started to work on this
- 3. You need to give this more time.

PRODUCT SELF-ASSESSMENT

Questions	1	2	3
How well do you understand what product(s) you sell, to whom you sell them, and why your customers buy them?			
How relevant is your product in today's market?			
How well do you understand your competition?			
In a crowded marketplace, how well do you understand your key differentiators?			
How able are you to adjust your product to meet changing customer needs?			
Are adequate quality control processes in place?			
Do you have the right people with the right skills in place to deliver your product?			
How confident are you that you have legal, approved-by-regulators, protection for your product or idea?			
How well is your business prepared to handle growth?			
How strong is your inventory and scalability to meet customer demand?			
How complete and current is your plan for the evolution of your product and your company?			
How is your product priced in the market for your growth and profitability?			

SALES SELF-ASSESSMENT

Questions	1	2	3
How effective is your sales team recruitment process?			
How well-defined are your interview and onboarding processes and how closely do you adhere to them?			
Do you have an effective training process and materials in place?			
How good are you at retaining your top salespeople?			
Do you have a margin in place, that is, a must-have minimum to achieve on every deal?			
Do you have financial incentives in place for performance?			
Do you clearly know what makes your product stand out?			
How well-defined, understood, and followed is your account planning process?			
How well-defined and followed is your sales cycle?			
How much knowledge do you have about the most effective way to sell your products?			
How well do your sales teams close sales?			
How well do you manage your sales pipeline?			
How well-defined is your supply chain, from sourcing through distribution?			
How skillful are you at identifying reference customers who can help your sales?			

CUSTOMER SELF-ASSESSMENT

Questions	1	2	3
How good are you at knowing who your customers are?			
How extensive is your knowledge of what your customers think of your product?			
How well do you understand what you want your customer experience to be?			
If your customers differ by channel or type, do you have a strategy for each?			
How would you rate your customer service?			
How aware are you of what customer needs are not being met by your company?			
Do you understand your cost structure for products so that you can produce the best products at the most advantageous prices?			
Do you have a product pipeline?			
How aware are you of the cycle time for your products?			
How well does your cycle time accommodate scaling up?			
How aware are you of how your customers would rate their satisfaction with your company?			
Is your product delivery customer friendly?			
How aware are you of whether your customer wants to hear from you and at what frequency?			
How adept are you at sharing and applying customer feedback to improve your company?			

MARKETING SELF-ASSESSMENT

Questions	1	2	3
How well do you understand your brand?			
How unique is your brand?			
How well does your brand represent your entire family of products?			
How clearly are you conveying your brand in your current marketing efforts?			
How accommodating are you about solving problems for a customer?			
How well do you know your company's story?			
How clearly are you communicating that story in your current marketing efforts?			
How clear are you about which customers or businesses are the focus of your marketing strategies?			
Do you have developed personas about the customer base that can help guide your marketing?			
How integrated is your marketing with other parts of your company (e.g., sales, product, finance)?			
How clearly have you defined your marketing audiences by channel?			
Do you know how to reach, market to, and influence your customers?			
How well do you understand (i.e., measure) the			

effectiveness of your current marketing strategy?			
How would you rate your current marketing plan for such things as completeness and relevance?			
How would you rate your social media effectiveness?			

CHAPTER 3

THE PRODUCT QUADRANT

"Quality means doing it right when no one is looking."
Henry Ford

Your company likely began with a great idea. You or a group of individuals came up with something that you thought people would want to buy. Your heart is in it and you have made it your life passion to bring it to market. You may have quit your job to devote your full attention to it, you may have invested your entire savings or borrowed extensively. You have likely worked long hours with (initial) minimal return while your idea consumed your every waking moment. You may even have written and followed a business plan, obtained the needed funding, and then formed your company to develop and sell your great idea.

This chapter is intended to make you aware of the key questions you should be continually asking about your product. Having well-thought-out answers to these questions is critical to your business success.

Note: Many companies sell products and services. The authors throughout this book use the term "product" to apply to both products and services.

YOUR SOLUTION

What business are you in? What do you sell? The answers should be obvious, but it's good to be thinking continually about your business and product from a macro perspective. If you are in the coffee shop business, for example, thinking from the macro view would mean asking: am I selling just a cup of coffee or am I selling an inviting experience with an ambiance in which customers can read and work while they enjoy my finely magnificently brewed coffee?

Have you clearly identified the market you're in and who your customers are? Market segments (Figure 3-1) are well established and can help you define your target audiences. It's important to be clear about who your customer is because many of your business decisions (e.g., competitive analysis, pricing, product positioning) should be tailored to that type of person.

You need to continually think of your customer audience as holistically as possible because there are often "hidden customers" that are not apparent at first blush.

Segmentation	Explanation	Examples
Demographic	Quantifiable population characteristics (age, gender, income, education, socioeconomic status, family size or situation)	Young, upwardly mobile, prosperous professionals; dual income, no kids; graying, leisured, and moneyed; empty nester or full nester
Geographic	Physical location or region (country, state, region, city, suburb, postal code)	New Yorkers, urbanites, inner-city dwellers, suburbanites, small towners
Psychographic	Lifestyle, social, or personality characteristics (typically includes basic demographic descriptors)	Socially aware; traditionalists; conservatives; conscious of social causes; motivated by associated interests
Behavioral	Purchasing, consumption, or usage behavior (based on need, benefits that can be acquired, occasion for usage, purchase frequency, customer loyalty, buyer readiness)	Tech-savvy; heavy users; enthusiasts, early adopters; opinion leaders; luxury seekers; price conscious; quality conscious; time-poor

Figure 3-1. Market segmentation

For example, from a product perspective, what is it about your product that makes customers want to buy from you and what makes your product unique in the market? What is your differentiator? Rarely does a company sell a product in a completely new market or a brand-new product in an existing market. Usually, the company is joining others to compete for the same customer base, and because of this, the company needs to distinguish itself.

The message is that there will always be room for someone who does something in a different or better way. Also, change is fresh and fun. So, ask yourself, why would people buy my product over some other product?

Starbucks

When Starbucks began in 1971, many companies (called first wave) were doing well making and selling coffee. Starbucks became one of the first "second wave" coffee companies, and they initially differentiated themselves from other coffee serving venues in the United States by taste, quality, and customer experience. Despite joining an existing market, they distinguished themselves in it; today they operate nearly 28,000 locations worldwide.

IKEA

IKEA, which began as a single store in Agunnaryd, Sweden, is another example. Ingvar Kamprad founded the firm when he was seventeen, in 1943. Five years later, he entered the furniture business knowing that his toughest competitor, Gunnar Fabriker in Alvesta, had long sold furniture and so had Nilsson in Råshult. He found the simplest and cheapest way to convey goods from the factory to the customer was by direct purchase without middlemen. He combined mail order and furniture store in one, and as far as Kamprad knew, that business practice had not been put in place anywhere else. That uniqueness was one of the keys to IKEA's phenomenal growth; it has been the world's largest

MARKET RELEVANCE AND TIMING

Relevance answers the question of *why* your product is key. What problem does it solve or what issue does it address? What need does it meet? Think about the reasons people buy products and ask, Is my product relevant? Are there a hundred other solutions available? Am I confident that I have a solution to a market need?

> **Application Development Company**
>
> A small, software application development company has been in business for several years. They've developed an application that has been tested and is ready to sell. Their target market includes New York Stock Exchange traders who need up-to-the minute information about the market. Their application handles millions of transactions per second and requires processing of extremely large data sets. A barrier to sales has been the massive amount of storage a client needs to store the data the application requires. The advent of Cloud Computing has made the business case for their application extremely attractive. The world may now be ready for them.

Timing refers to *when* you bring your product to market and is critical to its success. One of the top reasons that companies flounder or fail is that their timing is not right. Are your customers ready for your product? Have you missed a window of opportunity? Or have you hit the

window, just right? The message is that your product is highly dependent on whether
the world is ready for it.

If your timing is early and you are confident about the future, you need to be patient. You can leverage your marketing efforts, conferences, and speaking engagements to get your message and build a community, and eventually, a market. Or, as in the example with the Cloud, a new business model may provide the boost you need. Find a way to keep some revenue flowing in by signing early adopters.

There are many benefits to being a "fast follower." For example, you can examine how another company went to market, who they approached, and, more importantly, what worked and what failed in their approach and products. If you can correct the failures and build on the successes, a fast-follower strategy can be the right way to proceed.

If you are late to the market, you need to be better than the rest. Create a lower cost structure and get the product right. Find some unique value you can add to your product or idea. To do this, use customer surveys, focus groups, and similar research methods to uncover the next big idea.

COMPETITION

"Victorious warriors win first and then go to war, while defeated warriors go to war first and then seek to win".
Sun Tzu

Competition is a contest or rivalry between two or more entities, individuals, economic groups, or social groups. Everyone is competing over scarce resources. The scarce resources for small businesses are customers, funding, and recognition in the marketplace as a provider a market leading solution. So, if competition is a rivalry and you compete in the market for position, you will need to plan your battle appropriately. One of the best books written about competition is *The Art of War* by Sun Tzu, published in the fifth century BC. Sun Tzu's strategies can help a company successfully compete in business by laying a plan, using resources, positioning troops, and leveraging scouts. The authors of this book strongly encourage the reader to read this book to put you in the right mindset to define your competitors and devise a plan to crush them.

> ## Blue Apron
> Delivery is the business area in which the New York City company Blue Apron stood head and shoulders above its competition. Founded in 2012, they began selling just twenty meal kits (recipes and ingredients). Matt Wadiak is the visionary behind the eclectic mix of recipes that rely on farm-fresh foods and spices. Today they are valued at $2 billion with 4,000 employees and sells 8 million meal kits a month.

Your immediately understandable competitors include companies that offer the same or similar products as you do, have geographic market areas that overlap with yours, and have similar price points. Competitors are also companies that offer products or services that are substitutes for yours. You need to keep a watchful eye on the industry to see who else could emerge as competition.

Complete a table like the one shown in Figure 3-2 to help see how you stand versus your competitors. List their names in the row below the Competition heading. For each row, mark a plus sign where you feel you are stronger than the competitor, a minus sign where you believe you are weaker, and an equal sign if neither of you has an advantage. Think about the functional elements of your product and the emotional elements, which could include influences that change your customers' lives and may have social impact. Together, these elements form your value. Please feel free to add other elements to this table that are unique to your business. These business areas were defined to generally cover most use cases.

From this look at your competition, a clear picture of your strengths and weaknesses should emerge, which can help you think of ways to be different and better. You might see, for example, that your business stands out over competitor A's business because you supply a full line of products and they don't. Your edge over competitor B might be that you provide services after sales and they don't. You might also realize that your product is of higher quality than competitor C's product and you give a money-back guarantee, which they don't offer.

The multiple rows of the table provide a reminder that there are more reasons than your base product function that can set you apart from your competition. If needed, add, delete, or revise the Business Area items shown so that the list captures the most important aspects of your company. Every row provides an area in which you can be an innovator. Another important task is to analyze what the market is saying about you and your competitors. This will be very helpful when you are trying to differentiate your product and/or services from your competitors' offerings.

Business Area	You Relative to Competitors (+, –, =)		
	A	B	C
Product line			
Base product function			
Development processes and life cycle			
Cost and cost structures (e.g., supply chain)			
Regulatory impacts and compliance			
Price			
Quality and reliability			
Service			
Sales			
Delivery			
Channels			
Holistic client experience			
Promotion			
Marketing			
Timing			
Geographic areas in which product is sold			

Figure 3-2. Your company versus competition

PRODUCT EVOLUTION

"It is not the strongest of the species that survives, nor the most intelligent, but the one most response to change"

Charles Darwin

Evolution is the gradual development of an entity, especially from a simple to a more complex form. Product evolution is a continuous process that includes strategy, organization, concept generation, market plan creation, evaluation, and commercialization. It seems to have an inevitable course. Products change over time, even though they are still serving the same purpose: Think of the bicycle, the automobile, the phone, and the computer. It is difficult to name a product other than the paper clip that hasn't changed dramatically over the years. As you develop and sell your product, you're going to need to be prepared to adjust to keep moving in a direction that your customers embrace. Most coffee shops began by offering only black coffee. One day, customers wanted lattes, so the way the coffee was made changed and the product offerings were broadened.

Product evolution is an artificial process rather than a natural process. Its trajectory is very hard to predict accurately because (1) past trends do not always repeat themselves as time goes by and (2) so many different factors are involved in bringing about a change, including technology advancements, customer needs, consumer habits, and market pressures, to name a few.

Something else to think about is that different trends occur in different places, whether other neighborhoods, other cities, or other countries. These trends may not have been introduced into your market. You need to be a student of your product, constantly focusing on research and attempting to anticipate where the market will potentially go.

QUALITY CONTROL

"Quality is not an act; it is a habit"

Aristotle

Quality control (also called quality management) is a system for verifying and maintaining the desired level of quality your customers expect of your product and meeting the standards that apply to your industry. It involves careful planning, testing, continued inspection, and corrective action, as required.

Quality control levels, types, and complexities vary by industry and from business to business, so you should be aware of the most important standards in your industry and comply with them. Restaurants, for example, need to ensure that food storage, handling, and cooking processes conform to food safety guidelines and regulations. Companies that develop software applications require a robust testing process to ensure that reliability, performance, and scalability are meeting the intended design points. These companies usually have separate development, testing, and production environments for simulating how customers will use an application.

The ISO 9000 family of quality management systems standards was first published in 1987 by the International Organization for Standardization; it has evolved over the years. It is designed to help companies ensure that they meet the needs of customers and other stakeholders while also meeting statutory and regulatory requirements related to their product. ISO 9000 deals with the fundamentals of quality management systems, including the seven quality management principles upon which the family of standards is based. ISO 9001 deals with the requirements that organizations wishing to meet the standards must fulfill. Third-party certification bodies provide independent confirmation that organizations are meeting the requirements. Over one million organizations worldwide are independently certified, making ISO 9001 one of the most widely used quality management tools in the world today.

Dell Computing

In 2003, Dell introduced a disk drive-based MP3 player and details of a partnership with music download company Musicmatch. It flourished for a time, but in 2006 they withdrew it from the market. Apple owns the music player market. What happened? Dell seemed to become so focused on product quality that they lost touch with their customers. The message is that being the best at something may not guarantee success. Don't become fixated on making your product perfect, because perfect can be the enemy of good. Know what quality levels you must meet and then attain them. Less than perfect may, at times, be all you need to be.

DELIVERY SERVICES

Developing your product requires one set of skills but delivering the final product to your customers requires a separate set. It is critical that you have properly trained, geographically positioned, and available-when-needed delivery services personnel.

When rolling out a new product, your focus should be on getting customer adoptions and market traction. Aim to present and deliver your solution in the best and most efficient way to drive repeat business and generate reference clients that lead to new deals.

LEGAL PROTECTION

How do you ensure that your product or idea for a product won't be stolen? This is a valid concern from the beginning, because to get your idea off the ground, you need to enlist others, such as investors, partners, employees, and vendors. How can you communicate and promote your idea without someone taking it?

Intellectual property is a broad category of protections for human thoughts and ideas. It includes copyrights, patents, and trademarks, among others. The goal of the intellectual property stipulations is to encourage people to generate ideas and profit from them without having the competition steal them.

A patent is an option, but patents cost money, anywhere from hundreds to thousands of dollars. If your product is at the idea stage, know that you cannot patent or copyright an idea. After you have developed your idea into a design, then you can patent the design.

A nondisclosure agreement is good for those who feel they are onto something new, need to share it with others, and want to protect their idea from being stolen. Before going this route, you should ensure that your idea is like none other that exists, or you may quickly lose credibility when a person to whom you have explained your idea comes across something similar. If you encounter someone who is reluctant to sign a nondisclosure agreement, you should not work with that person.

Whether or not you go the patent or nondisclosure route, it is a good idea to mark your documents and presentations, or anything made of paper related to your idea, as CONFIDENTIAL so you can claim ownership for your work. You can also add copyright symbols (© 2019 William Bierds) and trademark claims (™) to logos, which help to establish that you are claiming copyright and trademark protection of your work. This legally prevents someone from making a physical copy of a business plan or summary of your idea.

Some experts in this area say not to worry too much about the risk of someone stealing your idea. The difference maker for successful businesses is not the idea alone. It is the implementation of the idea and a commitment to delivering the products that make the biggest difference.

SCALABILITY

Successful business growth depends on a scalable business model that allows for expansion and revenue growth while minimizing increases in operational costs. Even if you're not ready to grow now, there are things you can do to set yourself up for scalable growth and success in the future:

Build a solid foundation: Review your business to see what functions are inefficient or uneconomical and make it your goal to streamline them as much as possible so that your attention can remain focused on growth-related activities and your core strengths. Scalable business owners are experts at leveraging outside resources. Outsource as many of the noncore tasks associated with running your business as you can. Build a team of freelancers to do what *they* do best so you can concentrate on what *you* do best. Be sure to include noncompete clauses in their contracts.

Focus on scalable business solutions: It can be tempting to go with the quick (or cheap) fix. Money, time, and expertise can be in short supply, and investing in basic solutions that don't require a significant financial investment or learning curve can seem like the wisest solution at first. Resist the temptation to piece together a myriad of inexpensive and inadequate options and think ahead to determine what will serve your business best in the future. A forward-thinking mindset can help you avoid the common small business trap of having a patchwork maze of systems that just aren't getting the job done. Think the way the owner of a business 10 times larger than your current one would think. Choose solutions that will serve what is *and* what may come.

Take time for strategic planning: Strategic planning is the link between a great idea and true success and growth. More a philosophy of operation than a one-time event, it requires ongoing attention to detail and an investment of time. Knowing your business inside and out can prepare you to deal with challenges and help you leverage opportunities to scale. Develop a series of quarterly and annual priorities, a mission that sets the tone for the next 3 to 5 years of operation, and a goal to keep you reaching for success.

Be patient: A path of slow and steady growth is much more sustainable—and scalable—in the long run.

CUSTOMER SATISFACTION

"Do what you do so well that they will want to see it again and bring their friends"

Walt Disney

The best way to assess what customers think of your product is by asking them. Obtaining feedback can be as simple as talking to them face to face as they leave your store or office or as complex as spending thousands of dollars to hire an agency to conduct a survey for you. Other ways include phoning customers and emailing or mailing a survey to them. No matter which route you choose, be careful not to invade their privacy or be an irritant. Know that it's best to obtain feedback when the experience is fresh in your customer's mind. If you have a business Facebook page, you can have a forum where customers can share their opinions without you sending them a formal survey. Remember also that every interaction you have with a customer provides a chance to obtain feedback and win a long-time loyalty to your company.

One of your main reasons for surveying is finding a customer's answer to two key questions: (1) Will you buy from me again? and (2) Would you recommend that others buy from me? The most important aspect of the customer satisfaction survey is what you do with the feedback. Investigate valid suggestions; fix, if you can, the things your customers have complained about; don't change what they like; and improve in areas that mean the most to them. Let those who provide feedback know that you appreciate their time and comments. Also, after you make changes because of survey input, let people know that their feedback has been listened to and acted upon.

CHAPTER 4

THE SALES QUADRANT

"Setting goals is the first step in turning the invisible into the visible."

Tony Robbins

In the previous chapter, we talked about the importance of your product. It certainly is important, but without sales your product is just a good idea. Revenue from sales provides the fuel that keeps your business going and growing. Without it, you will cease to exist. Sales also indicate whether your company has purpose by addressing a need. No sales—or declining sales—means that something is wrong, and what is wrong could be one of many things. For example, your product may not meet a need, your marketing may not be promoting the product correctly, or the sales process may need to be adjusted.

Your sales team provides the "feet on the street" that are walking your company along the path to success. Salespeople can see what is and is not working long before it shows up on a quarterly report. Some companies underinvest in their sales quadrant, treating it like an afterthought to be handled after managers solve the manufacturing, distribution, and financing issues. The best sales forces are made up of professional, well-compensated individuals who are supported with a strong marketing effort and empowered to act. They serve key client interests with marketing support, money, and time. They have strong personal relationships with key customers. They, along with others in your company who interact directly with customers, truly are your business.

This chapter will help you assess whether you have plans and processes in place to make the sales quadrant of your company as successful as it can be, from (1) hiring the right people and getting them to be productive as quickly as possible, (2) developing account plans, (3) following a clearly defined sales cycle that ends in deal closure, and (4) managing your pipeline effectively. We'll begin with hiring your salespeople.

HIRING, TRAINING, AND RECRUITING SALESPEOPLE

Your success hinges on your ability to (1) recruit, interview, and hire the right salespeople, (2) get them to be productive as quickly as possible, and (3) set clear expectations for them that align with and support company goals. If you are a relatively small company—fewer than 50 employees, for example—each person you hire can take the company on a wrong turn. The larger your company, the less the risk of that happening, but the more difficult it can be to spot and address a mediocre or poor performance.

Companies can make a myriad of mistakes when hiring their salespeople. To make the fewest mistakes and have the greatest chance of bringing in people who are right for a company, there must be a well-defined process in place that includes everybody involved in the hiring process. A clearly communicated, effective hiring process brings in quality people who will fit into your company's culture and are likely to absorb future training so they can perform in accordance with your business beliefs. Following the process helps you hire people who will fit in the best and lays a solid foundation on which to build your company's success.

The hiring process begins with you identifying a need and ends with a fully productive employee who satisfactorily meets the need.

1. RECRUITING

Ideally, you may be able to hire someone in your network of business associates who you know already, a person who has a proven track record, understands your business, and can demonstrate value quickly. If you go this route, be sure to have these individuals go through the same interview process, with all key managers, as any other candidate. The person must also complete training and be prepared to adjust to the culture of the firm. If you don't see signs of a willingness to assimilate, cut the ties early.

Recruiting is a necessary evil. Your network is good, but it is not going to fill all your needs. The most critical aspect of recruiting is to be specific about what the position entails and what skills and experiences the person must have. Simply saying you want to hire a great salesperson is not enough. You want to be clear about what the person would be selling and to whom. For example, the person might need experience in and a track record of selling to companies in a certain industry of a certain size and to employees with specific job titles. The person selling $500,000 solutions to an executive in a large company needs different experiences and skills than the person selling $5,000 products to a mid-level manager in a small business.

As you recruit, take an objective look at your company. Why would a salesperson want to work for your company? Consider things such as compensation, the benefits package, flexible hours or work-at-home options, chances to develop new skills and advance upward in the company, profit-sharing programs, and bonuses. Most important to keep in mind is that top salespeople want to work in an upbeat, team-focused environment. The culture of a company attracts people and retains them.

2. INTERVIEWING

It is best to follow a formal, repeatable interview process. The process that Google uses is described in the book *How Google Works* by Eric Schmidt and Jonathan Rosenberg. At Google, every candidate is interviewed five times. The interviewers ask "fixed" interview questions that address areas about which they want to hear from the candidate. After the interview is complete, the interviewers meet, compare notes, and must come to a unanimous hiring position regarding the candidate to extend an offer. The interviewers should be open and honest. Do not let a senior person win the day just because of being senior. Remember, you are building a culture, and mistakes can be hard to fix.

In addition to interviews, candidates should have a chance to meet informally with some of the people with whom they would work. This helps candidates to get a feel for their coworkers and helps your employees to get a feel for the persons who may be hired. Current employees will appreciate sharing their views on their work and the company with prospects. This all gives the existing employees a stake in the game. You may not want them to have a final say in the hiring decision, but you should welcome their input. If a candidate is hired, you might assign a mentor from among the coworkers involved during the interview stage.

Whether you own a large company with a human resources department or a small company with only a few employees, your interviews should include questions that help you decide the following:

- Does a candidate have the skills to do the job?
- Does a candidate have a track record of success?
- How well does a candidate handle pressure?
- How well will a candidate fit into the team and your company?

Does a candidate have the skills to do the job?

Determining this may be the most straightforward part of the interview. You will have seen the person's resume, so you'll have a clear understanding of the person's education, experiences, and skills. Ask open-ended questions (not to be answered "yes" or "no") to find out more about the person's background, such as

- What are some specific examples of previous sales experiences? What would you do the same? What would you do differently?
- When you were the sales manager for company XYZ, how did you go about creating your account plans?
- I see you have closed on several large deals. Tell me about one of your more challenging and satisfying ones.
- What is your understanding of this company's sales cycle, and how does it compare with what you've done in the past?

Listen carefully to the answers. How confident is the person? How complete are the answers? Does the candidate answer the question you asked, or does the answer become redirected to a different topic?

Does a candidate have a track record of success?

Nearly every applicant's resume lists trips won, quotas met, and other achievements. What you really need to know is what actions were taken to get to the achievements. Was the applicant the lead person? If so, did the applicant direct people to do things or did the applicant do the work alone? By exploring the awards, quotas, and achievements, you may find holes in the narrative. It is much easier to not hire someone who is stretching the truth than it is to fire the person once hired.

How well does a candidate handle pressure?

Most salespeople perform well during the "good times" (i.e., when the economy is flourishing, when a quota is being met, and when their accounts are prospering). You want a salesperson who can also function well during the not-so-good times. Ask questions that will give you insights into how the person will perform under pressure or put the person in a somewhat "uncomfortable" position:
- Tell me about a stressful situation that occurred repeatedly on your last job and how you handled it.

- Which coworker at your last job did you get along with least well? What did you do about it?
- Why do you consider yourself better for this job than all the other candidates?"
- What's a significant mistake that you made, how did you correct it, and what did you learn from it?

The important thing to watch for is how directly and completely the applicant answers your questions. Beware of candidates who claim they have never been in a stressful situation.

How well will a candidate fit into the team and your company?

Among equally qualified candidates, this is the most important attribute. You need someone who will fit in with the team and be a productive member, someone who will add to the team and not be a distraction. Be careful, though. You aren't looking for the "nicest" person. You are looking for the best fit. Here are examples of questions you could ask to help you see how the person would fit into your company:
- What do you see as this company's strengths, and what changes do you think would improve its sales and productivity? How do you feel you could contribute to this improvement?
- What do you see as the greatest contributions you can make to improve the company's success?

- How do you see your career developing in the next few years, and how will you accomplish that in this company?

Your company has its own culture, as do individual groups within your company. The company culture is constantly evolving. You need to consider where you are in this process and hire accordingly. For example, when a company first begins, nearly everybody is "winging it," pounding the pavement, knocking on doors, and trying to get people to buy their product. They initially need a super salesperson who works best "going it alone." As the company matures and grows, however, the company still needs excellent salespeople, but it may need more team players who follow a disciplined process. As you ask questions and listen to the responses, consider how well a candidate will fit in with your company's culture.

3. EXTENDING THE OFFER

Sales hiring decisions are some of the most important business decisions you will make. After the interviews, assess what you've heard. When you are ready to make an offer, take a minute to consider the following questions to help you be sure you are making the right choice. These questions assume that you have determined the person has the right skills, will work well under pressure, and will fit in with coworkers.

- Is the person not only right for the job but right for the good of the entire company?
- Is the person a self-starter? How much handholding and management time do you anticipate the person needing after going through the onboarding phase to become a productive employee?
- Are you about to hire a potential superstar or a strong supporting player? You need superstars, but your company's success rides just as much on the steady players who are dependable and do good workday in and day out.
- How well does the person know the industry (e.g., government, telecommunications, entertainment) in which the person will be selling?

4. DEVELOPTING A PRODUCTIVE EMPLOYEE

It is important to set the expectation that the employee is responsible for learning what needs to be learned. The company can provide classroom and web-based training and papers to read, but at the end of the day, it is the time the employee spends watching YouTube, reading books, surfing the web, and more that will bring the best results.

The time between the salesperson's start date and the date of becoming fully productive represents the *opportunity cost of a company's onboarding process*. During this window, the employee is not producing revenue or helping you achieve your corporate revenue goal. The turnover of salespeople is just under 40%, and 29% of the 40% are new hires, so this topic requires time and attention. An effective onboarding program is one that minimizes the size of the learning window so that salespeople move into a revenue production mode more quickly. It is easy to say this, but it is much more difficult to put it into practice.

Some companies refer to the assimilation process as "new hire training." New hire training typically comes in one of two forms. (1) There is the fire hose program, whereby the company throws everything it has at the neophyte salesperson during the first week of employment. Retention is minimal. Frustration is high. (2) There is also the osmosis program; this approach includes letting the new salesperson figure everything out unassisted. It's usually based on the thought that if this new person is a great salesperson, he or she will figure it out and won't need any help. In both cases, companies are often unpleasantly surprised by the high turnover and underperformance of their salespeople.

Instead of either of these approaches, we recommend a personalized onboarding program that you can build from your answers to the following questions:

- What does the person need to know to do the job?
- When does the person need to know it?
- How will you verify that the person knows what is needed to do the job successfully?

What does the person need to know to do the job?
The first step is to identify all the things a salesperson needs to know to be successful in your company. The list is going

to be long. That is to be expected. No detail is too small. Also, don't worry about prioritizing the list. Here are examples of topics your sales hires should know:

- Company: Mission, purpose, history, culture, organizational structure, policies, human resources, regulations, environmental issues, and other related topics
- Offering: Product, product positioning, service, solution, components, value proposition, design, attributes, key clients, business partners, third-party thought leadership, and use cases
- Sales related: Networking, negotiating, deal closing, and account planning
- Industry: Regulations and terminology
- Competition: Their offerings, key clients, value propositions, partners, and positioning (how you are different and how you beat the competitors)
- Corporate processes: Mastering the complete set of steps from first call to contact, account planning, objection handling, and role playing
- Sales process: All internal processes related to sales and any cross-functional processes; they include talent management (interviewing), sales engineering (demos), customer support, sales operations, marketing (lead follow-up and field-driven events), and sales management (pipeline review, coaching, and deal desk)
- Systems: Customer relationship management, forecasting, knowledge management, internal email, requests for customer materials, expense accounts, and

other corporate support systems that may get in the salesperson's way

When does the person need to know it?

Now that you have a comprehensive list, resist the temptation to turn on the fire hose. The person likely doesn't need to know everything today, nor can you effectively teach that way. With adult learning, it is important to generate chunks of information in such a way that the "student" can learn them. Hour after hour of lecturing or reading will accomplish little. Each segment should be 60 to 90 minutes at most if you plan for the new hire to retain the information. There should also be a logical succession to the program. Each day and week, the new hire should be building a foundation. Solid foundations lead to a long tenure and strong results. Plot each of the identified topics on a weekly schedule. From there, you can break it down into a daily program. Completing the training successfully should be required for each employee.

How will you verify that the person knows what is needed to do the job successfully?

This is the area where many new-hire programs fall short. You invest significant time and resources in the new sales hires, but how do you evaluate their assimilation? Some employees get off to a fast start, get complacent, lose focus, and don't sustain a good performance. It is best to clearly set and monitor 3-month, 6-month, and 9-month goals for them as they get up to speed and engage with their clients. Make it clear that they are accountable for reaching their goals and provide constructive feedback as needed.

5. DEVELOPING AN ONBOARDING PROGRAM

An onboarding program you develop can help turn a new employee into a productive employee in a planned way rather than an overwhelming or haphazard one. There is no standard answer for how long an onboarding program should be. It is based on the level of complexity of the sales environment. It could be days for some companies and weeks or months for others. One of the added benefits of an onboarding program is that it can help you determine how a person is doing early in the first few months on the job. Should a person not be a good fit, it's best for the person and for you to address the problems sooner rather than later. As a condition of full employment, the training needs to be done. Your onboarding program can consist of one or more of the following types of training:

- New employee orientation
- Mentoring
- On-the-job training
- Formal training

New Employee Orientation: New employee orientation is the process for welcoming a new employee into your company. The goal of the orientation is to help the person feel welcomed and part of your company plus share with the person the core information that all employees need to know. Depending on the job responsibilities and the person's experience, topics will vary, but they typically are the following:

- Company history and culture
- Organization charts (who's who)
- An introduction to each department in the company
- Benefits and benefits eligibility
- The work environment
- Safety

Ensure the new hire has a world-class first day. Many new hires express dissatisfaction with their first day because their manager was too busy to give them the required attention. The disgruntled participants said their first-day meetings were cut short, they ended up getting shuffled off to others, and they went home after day one feeling disengaged.

Mentoring: Mentoring is a formal or informal relationship established between an experienced, knowledgeable employee and a new employee. The purpose of a mentor is to help the new employee quickly absorb the organization's culture. Mentoring can also help an employee learn what is needed to succeed in the job and role as employee. A mentor can serve as a sounding board as the new employee is assimilated into the company and can help evaluate their progress.

On-the-Job Training: On-the-job training is training at the place of work while a person is doing the actual job. Often, an experienced employee or the mentor provides this training.

Formal Training: Research says that more than 70% of learning on the job occurs informally. Companies, however, have little control over the topics and presentation of material in informal training, so although informal training has its place, formal training is a more established and trusted way for employees to learn new skills and obtain information needed to do their job. Formal learning programs are structured and outcome based. Formal training is a perfect approach when it has set standards on what will be taught and is consistent in the material and knowledge presented. Formal training can be classroom based or provided via webinars, screen-sharing sessions, or interactive live web events. If you have neither the budget nor the expertise to develop your own formal training program, you can hire a training consultant firm to help you determine what you need, develop it, and teach it.

Personalized Onboarding Plan: After you understand what the new employee needs to know and do, when they need to know and do it, and how you will provide it, you can develop onboarding plans tailored to individual employees or groups of employees.

6. RETAINING GOOD SALESPEOPLE

Good salespeople leave companies for valid reasons: Their quotas are either unclear or unreasonable; they don't have a good customer base; the products they sell have shortcomings; or they don't have the sales support to help them deliver on their sales. Some of the salespeople treat their work as a job; others become passionate about what they do and who they work for. To attain the latter, be honest with them. Ensure they understand how they will be measured and provide timely feedback. Feedback in the moment—right after a call that didn't (or did) go well, a deal lost (or won)—has a better chance of assimilation than feedback delayed. Not everyone is motivated by the same things, so know what drives each person and do your best to provide it. Show your employees how attaining their goals ties into and contributes to your company's meeting its overall goals. Ultimately, pay them well; provide good benefits and perks; foster an upbeat, fun work environment; and show them (actions speak louder than words) that you value them and their contributions.

SALES ACCOUNT PLANS

Sales account planning brings together critical information about your customers, your competitors, and your strategy to win business. Account plans provide a structure to determine what's important and what's not when pursuing customers. As competition in markets increases, account plans become critical to reaching goals and achieving growth.

Account plans vary in length, from one page to more than fifty. A longer plan isn't necessarily a better plan. The best plan is one that creates a healthy tension between being clear and action oriented and having enough detail to describe the strategy. The six components below are included in most plans. Determine the level of detail that works best for your culture, remembering that time spent gathering insight and planning specific actions is better than having teams that do not know information or than scrambling to make a plan at the last minute.

- *Profile and Position* gives an overview of the account and the strengths and weaknesses of the relationships. It answers the question, where are we now?
- *Needs Mapping and Alignments* describes your understanding of the customer needs and the organizational alignments of your team to the account. This section answers the questions, who are the buyers? How do we (your employees) align?
- *Goals and Strategy* describes your overall objectives for the account and how you will reach your goal. It answers

the questions, what are our objectives? What's our overall direction for achieving them?
- *Action Plan* takes each component of the goal and develops a tactical plan to achieve the goal. It answers the question, what is our plan to achieve each opportunity?
- *Team Support* describes how your organization needs to come together across functions to support the account plan. It answers the question, what internal commitments do we need?
- *Performance Dashboard* sets milestones and tracks your progress in reaching those milestones; it also helps identify any adjustments that need to be made. It answers the questions, how have we performed? How should we adjust?

Account plans provide a vehicle for ensuring that your teams are aligned in the effort to reach well-defined goals. This helps employees have a consistent understanding of what they are doing, why they are doing it, and how they support the big picture. Also, account plans help you set down the details that support a large goal (i.e., you shouldn't have a $100-million revenue plan without knowing the details of how it will be accomplished) and which individual accounts may be involved (e.g., if you have 12 accounts that are going to produce $10 million each, you want to know how you'll support them in total with finances, planning, service, and product support).

> ## Andrews Distributing
> Andrews Distributing, one of the largest beer distributors in the United States, began following a structured account planning process. It collected large amounts of data about its customers' buying habits and, based on what was learned, changed its sales coverage model. That year, says Mike Barnes, executive vice president, the company had twelve consecutive months of share growth—a first for Andrews. "We're now in our third year, and as we have improved in account planning, we've seen our market share grow," Barnes explains. The company is now in its thirty-fourth consecutive month of share growth, which is virtually unheard of in its industry.

Though it takes time to draw up an account plan, it is well worth the effort. For example, as you enable the sales teams to create an account planning process, continue to emphasize that account planning isn't about the document; it's about knowing the client needs, the innovative ideas that could meet those needs, a committed plan to address the needs, and the discipline of ownership and execution by the team. The plan will also document the results of much hard work, and it will continue to evolve as the teams succeed.

The revenue goal for the account is the foundation for the account plan. It identifies your starting point from a market perspective, a customer perspective, and your own perspective.

TYPES OF ACCOUNT PLANS

Account plans are not one-size-fits-all. Your sales strategy, sales process, and revenue goals will determine which type of account plan is right for each customer. Following are the most common types:

- *Strategic:* Strategic plans are for large, complex accounts, typically those that represent large revenue deals. The plans are designed to grow the accounts.
- *Tactical:* Not all accounts warrant a comprehensive strategic account plan. Tactical plans are good for companies when the bulk of their revenue comes from midsized accounts. Tactical plans are simple and short, but they force sales teams to think through how they're going to achieve their goals.
- *Pursuit:* Pursuit plans are for new customers, even those so new that business is not yet officially being conducted with them and about whom information is limited. Structurally, a pursuit plan is the same as a strategic account plan, but it includes more work and time for gathering needed information, specifically about buyers associated with the account.

ENSURING THAT ACCOUNT PLANNING WORKS

To work, account plans must be reviewed, followed, and updated regularly. Creating them is not a one-time event. Ideally, account planning will fit within your company's strategic planning cycle. For a company in a fiscal year, planning probably needs to start early in the first quarter to allow enough cycle time for developing the plan. You don't want account planning to become a fire drill or a process you have to shortcut. A good account planning cycle will include an annual kick-off meeting and some homework (e.g., completing the first three sections of the plan) before the account planning meeting.

After the plan is approved, the account team should be held responsible for its action items, which should be referred to and updated throughout the year, as necessary. When the new year starts, the account plan is refreshed, and the cycle begins again.

Your sales teams need to be motivated to make account planning a habit. Some of the best motivators include incentive pay tied to account plans, recognition, and reward programs, and spotlighting the connection between winning deals and following an account plan.

SALES CYCLE

The sales cycle (Figure 4-1) is the process that your company's sales teams follow when selling a product to a customer. It encompasses all activities associated with closing sales. A well-developed, well-managed sales cycle is critical to the health of any business. Although all sales cycles vary in phases and length, most will have the following elements:

- *Prospecting:* Finding new prospects to fill the sales pipeline is a vital first step. Your marketing activities create leads that your sales teams follow up on. Your network can be of significant help during this phase, too. Reach out to family, friends, and your contacts on social media (LinkedIn and Facebook friends). Build opportunities from all you know, even those you may not think can help you. You never know everyone your network knows.
- *Understand customers and their needs:* You can only determine whether your product is a good fit if you truly

understand your prospect's business and needs. Equip your sales reps with the questions and resources they need to uncover the right information.

- *Initiate contact:* Different approaches work better for different industries and companies of various sizes. Often, the first contact is a phone call, an email, or a piece of physical mail.
- *Develop the sales plan:* Your sales team works with the customer to develop plans that are linked to the customer's business environment and needs. The plan also addresses the company's pain points or compelling reasons to act.
- *Present the offer:* This phase of the sales cycle is critical. Your sales team needs to present its offer as a solution to the customer's needs. They should tailor their proposal to the information they have gathered in the previous phases of the sales cycle.
- *Manage objections:* Understanding the likely objections, such as price and timing, and equipping your sales team to handle them appropriately will increase your win rate and speed up your sales process.
- *Close the sale:* In this phase, the sales team drives the deal to a close and gets the prospect's signature on the dotted line.
- *Implement well and collect referrals:* Smooth and successful product implementation is crucial and key to earning you repeat sales and new leads you can start driving through the sales cycle.

CLOSING DEALS

The way consumers make purchasing decisions is constantly changing, so it's important to continually reevaluate your sales strategy. Selling any type of product can be a fine line to walk. Below are some of the most effective behaviors that help sales teams close their sales faster:

- *Identify the decision maker:* No matter what industry you are in, knowing the decision maker is crucial to a successful close. The best-case scenario is that your sales team has a good working relationship with the decision maker and those who influence that person. The decision maker should either be the person who holds the budget or one who can influence the budget holder. After you have the key people in the company believing that your product is right for them, it's critical to know what the budget timeline is, where the windows of funding opportunity are, what flexibility they have with their budget, and if there is money outside the budget that has been set aside for emergency purposes.
- *Create a sense of urgency:* Attach a deadline to the deal to help give clients an incentive to commit. Whether it's a discount or something free, make them feel as if they have the upper hand. This does not mean you should rush the customer; it simply means trying to add a little extra reason why your product is the right choice, and the right choice right now.
- *Overcome objections:* Preparing the sales presentation to address and overcome potential objections can speed up

any deal. By having an outline of anticipated problems and a thoughtful analysis of the risks (called a landmine map), your sales team can be prepared to handle any resistance that might arise.

- *Know the competition:* Knowing the areas where you are more competitive than your competition can lead to that quick close. Your sales team should do their research and make sure they know what your product can do that the competitor's product can't. This is oftentimes the biggest selling point, so the team doesn't want to ignore it.

SALES PIPELINE MANAGEMENT

A sales pipeline is a queue that contains all your sales opportunities in each of the stages of your sales cycle. The sales pipeline is typically shown visually to help you see what deals are where in the cycle. Sales pipeline management is the tracking and management of every sales opportunity through every stage to a successful close. Effective pipeline management has been shown to contribute significantly to revenue and company growth. Having a sales pipeline is important for reasons other than financial ones, as well:

- *Accurate forecasting:* Pipelines provide a look into each sales rep's activity, how close each rep is to making a quota, and in the aggregate, how near or far the whole team is from meeting the target quota. Using the information generated by the sales team, it's easier to forecast the revenues in 30, 60, and 90 days (or beyond). Knowing when you'll be closing sales and what those sales will be is critical to other company departments, such as finance, operations, and manufacturing.
- *Targeted resource allocation:* By understanding where you are at each pipeline stage for each customer or opportunity, you can take steps to allocate resources to help close business deals. Sales managers can determine which deals are critical and whether they'll need more time and oversight.

- *Effective sales team management:* At each stage there are actions for successfully finishing that stage and keeping the opportunity moving through the pipeline. Tracking key metrics frequently means that sales managers can identify and ease challenges for each rep before they impede sales.
- *Increased deal closure speed:* If it's taking too long to move opportunities from stage to stage, tracking data will make that apparent. For example, let's say your annual sales goal per salesperson is $5 million dollars. If 50% of your sales team has reached only $1 million dollars in sales 6 months into the sales year, it means you should look at individual performances and take steps to make improvements based on the data you've gathered.
- *Increased total deal volume, size, and revenue:* You want the number of opportunities to grow and the size of those opportunities and the dollar amount they generate to keep growing, too. A sales pipeline illuminates when to spend less energy on specific types of opportunities, what to remove from the process, and which situations to pursue more vigorously.

A well-managed sales pipeline is about continuously improving the process itself and honing the skills of your salespeople. Everyone's aim should be to keep deals in the pipeline moving as quickly as possible from one stage to the next toward sales closures.

CHAPTER 5

THE CUSTOMER QUADRANT

"There is only one boss. The customer. And he can fire everybody in the company from the chairman on down, simply by spending his money somewhere else."
Sam Walton

You can never place too much emphasis on your customers. Fulfilling their needs develops a loyalty and satisfaction that keeps them with you (i.e., repeat business) rather than moving on to your competitors. The term *customer life cycle* describes the progression of steps a customer goes through when considering, purchasing, and using a product and maintaining loyalty to it. The cycle involves getting a potential customer's attention, informing the customer about what you have to offer, turning a prospective into a paying customer, and keeping the customer over the long term.

The life cycle has four phases: marketing, acquisition, relationship management, and loss or churn:

Marketing (attract) phase: Time at which messages are sent to the target market of prospective customers; we describe this phase in Chapter 6, The Marketing Quadrant

Customer acquisition (sales) phase: Time at which prospective customers became actual customers by buying your product; we describe this phase in Chapter 4, The Sales Quadrant.

Relationship management (support and resell) phase: Time at which customers are nurtured, supported, and ideally inspired to not only continue to purchase more but also to serve as references and advocates

Loss and churn (categorize) phase: Time at which customers, for various reasons, choose not to buy from your company. In this phase you need to decide which lost customers are of most value and try to win back their business.

Figure 5.1 shows the customer life cycle. Customer retention truly is a cycle, and the goal is to get the customer to move through it again and again.

Throughout the life cycle, customer experience, customer service, and customer care are critical elements. Customer experience and customer care span all phases; customer service applies primarily during the relationship management phase. All three efforts contribute to delivering on your company's promises and building faithful, satisfied customers.

CUSTOMER EXPERIENCE

Customer experience is the total journey of a customer's interactions with your brand, from first discovering and
researching your products to using them. Customer experience involves how customers feel about your company overall and includes the emotional, physical, and psychological connections they have with it. The Disney Corporation, for example, places a premium on customer experience. It passionately strives to make sure that guests at Disneyland have an enchanting, memorable visit that begins the moment they enter The Magic Kingdom. All Disney employees are knowledgeable about, and committed to, providing this experience.

Companies are investing more than ever before in building a strong customer experience, and many expect to soon compete based on experience more than on price or quality. According to a portfolio of publicly traded companies drawn from the top 20% of brands in Forrester's Customer Experience Index, companies that invest in customer experience had greater stock price growth and higher total returns than a similar portfolio of companies drawn from the bottom 20% of brands. Customer experience, therefore, is more than a buzzword; it should be at the heart of everything a company does. It is a holistic approach that aims to cause customers to remember positive experiences every time they think of a company with which they did business.

CUSTOMER SERVICE

Customer service (also called customer support) includes activities provided before, during, and after a sale. Although it can take extra resources, time, and money, good customer service leads to customer satisfaction, which, in turn, generates positive word-of-mouth advertising for your business, keeps your customers happy, and encourages customers to purchase from you again. Customer service could be helping a customer choose the right product before making a purchase, but it most often starts after a purchase has been made and often is only used when a customer encounters a problem.

People who have a positive experience with a company's customer service department will likely tell two or three others about their experience. Conversely, a person who has had a bad customer service experience will likely tell between 9 and 20 people. Nearly 75% of customers who stop doing business with a company do so because they aren't satisfied with customer service.

For the customer quadrant to support your company's growth, you want to be sure you have thought through customer service and how to handle it. A key decision is whether you want to provide support yourself or hire a third party to do it. For a small company, a third party is an attractive option because it avoids the hiring of dedicated support employees.

Technology companies, for example, typically provide support at levels 1, 2, and 3. Level 1 support, often available via a toll-free phone number, is the first point of contact; personnel answer usage questions and solve relatively simple problems. Each call received by your support team provides an opportunity for them to win a customer's heart. Level 2 support personnel investigate and resolve the more difficult technical issues that are passed to them from Level 1 personnel. Level 3 support personnel need extensive technical skills for investigating the most challenging technical problems. There's much advice available on building the best support structure for your company.

CUSTOMER CARE

Customer care builds an emotional connection between your customer and your company. It involves truly caring for your customers, listening to their needs, and finding the right solution that will contribute significantly to their success. You want your customers to thrive from doing business with you. If you treat them well and are straightforward about what they need to do to be successful, you're going to become their trusted advisor, someone they will buy from again in the future.

As an example, at some point in the sales process, the client evolves from being a prospect to a very likely client. At that point, you should start getting the customer ready for what actions will be needed after the sale closes. For example, for an IT solution sale, you can get clients thinking about training, professional services, how they'll manage the environment, the costs associated with managing the environment, and testing of the total solution. Your willingness to watch out for the customer's best interests demonstrates that you are thinking about the customer's success more than just making the sale.

REFERENCES AND ADVOCATES

Customer references are persons willing to talk to one of your prospective clients and share their experiences with your company in a positive light. Their relationship with your company is typically a reactive one (i.e., they respond to your requests to take a call or write a case study). Customer advocates (or champions) are proactive in their promotion of your brand to prospective clients. They don't need a request from you first. They believe in your product and present their views publicly on their own to others (at an event, conference, or trade show for example). In today's world of social media, references and advocates don't sit idle. They might start talking about your products, services, and people on social media at any time. You can often spot a potential reference or advocate during the presales phase and lay the groundwork for asking the person to be one. You should focus on the benefits the *advocate* would gain rather than the benefits you and your company would gain.

There are three kinds of references and advocates: (1) those who explain why they made the decision to go with your product, (2) those who share details of the sales, purchase, and deployment process and how it went, and (3) those who have had the solution deployed for a given time and can talk about what they've accomplished, what business they've closed, and what costs they've saved. Customer references and advocates need to be nurtured and given something in return (e.g., invitations to events, complimentary dinners) for helping your company.

CUSTOMER FEEDBACK

Customer feedback is information coming directly from customers about the satisfaction or dissatisfaction they feel with your product. Customer comments and complaints given to your company are an important resource for improving and addressing the needs and wants of the customer. Feedback is often mistaken for criticism. What might be viewed as criticism can help you improve your company. As such, customer feedback is a tool for continued learning.

Obtaining customer feedback is most often associated with customer surveys. Surveys are valuable, but not all people take time to respond to them. Consider one or more other ways to obtain feedback, including:
- Feedback during a live chat session
- Feedback forms on your website
- Regular "how are we doing?" calls to your customers
- Email follow-ups to new customers;
- Monitoring of social media; and
- Feedback on your order confirmation pages.

Your customer service team likely knows more about what customers are struggling with than your product development team. This will negatively affect development if they're isolated from the feedback. A commitment to gathering, organizing, and sharing customer feedback with all in your company plays an important role in pushing your product and business forward.

THE CUSTOMER IS ALWAYS RIGHT

Lastly, remember that the customer is always right. Sometimes it is best to simply stay focused on the big picture and let minor annoyances go. Keep in mind that your customers helped make your business what it is today.

CHAPTER 6

THE MARKETING QUANDRANT

"Branding is what people say about you when you're not in the room."

Jeff Bezos

Your company may have the most innovative products in the market, but this will remain a best kept secret without effective marketing. You can't expect your business to thrive without it. In other words, if you build it, they still may not come. You must get out there and tell people who you are, why your product is different from the competition, and how to find you. Marketing includes everything you do to reach and persuade prospects. Your marketing should generate awareness, interest, and enthusiasm for your product. There is unlimited room for creativity and endless ways to accomplish this. Ultimately, your marketing results feed your sales process, where you close sales and get signed contracts. You don't need a marketing Ph.D. to be a good marketer. The process of building a plan that is tailored to your customers, sticking to it, and applying the time and resources it needs are the common secrets to success. The marketing process begins with brand and story; it is critical to establish each before you begin to market and sell.

YOUR BRAND

A brand is your logo, your website, and your tagline. It's your color scheme and your brand usage booklet. It's your building, your employees, your management team, and your culture. It's your products. It's your pricing model, and it's the way you do business. Your brand is what makes your company your company. When it's been formulated well, a brand changes the way consumers think about and interact with your business. Having a good brand eliminates the need to compete on price alone. All things being equal, the company with the stronger brand will win any sale, even if its products are more expensive.

Consumers pay a premium for brand name products. Why do people pay hundreds of dollars for a new pair of Nike shoes? They're just shoes, after all. It's not the shoe. It's the image of the brand. Nike makes you feel empowered. When you step into a pair of Nike shoes, you feel you can do anything. The company's tagline even says so: Just Do It. A good brand also implies changing customers' lives for the better. For example, one insurance company's brand assures customers that they are "in good hands with Allstate."

YOUR STORY

Every business has a story to tell, something that will connect potential customers to its brand. Company storytelling brings the history to life in the heads and hearts of customers and employees. The social meaning of your business becomes visible and tangible.

For all that companies gain as they grow, they often lose much of the intensity of the few founders who worked at the start-up stage. Foundational stories make for good marketing, and they also can serve as a good recruitment tool, connecting founders to incoming employees. They are particularly valuable when small companies reach the stage where they need to bring in outside professionals to help manage growth, yet don't want to diminish the "soul" of the company. Origin chapters define the firm's early values and heroes, and later chapters can showcase new employees who fill key gaps and enhance the culture.

Kentucky Fried Chicken

At age 40, Harland Sanders was running a service station in Kentucky, where he would also feed hungry travelers. Sanders eventually moved his operation to a restaurant across the street and featured a fried chicken so notable that he was named a Kentucky colonel in 1935 by Governor Ruby Laffoon. After closing the restaurant in 1952, Sanders devoted himself to franchising his chicken business. He traveled across the country, cooking batches of chicken from restaurant to restaurant, striking deals that paid him a nickel for every chicken the restaurant sold. In 1964, with more than 600 franchised outlets, he sold his interest in the company for $2 million to a group of investors. Today, Kentucky Fried Chicken's revenues are more than $20 billion annually.

TYPES OF MARKETING

Some people mistakenly equate marketing only with advertising. There is much more to marketing than that. Marketing can include some or all of the following:
- Websites
- Social media
- Business networking
- Advertisements
- Public relations
- Events
- Trade shows
- Influencers (includes analysts)
- Strategic partnerships

WEBSITES

In today's technology-based world, the first thing a potential customer or employee does is Google your company name. In a survey conducted by Clutch.co, only 64% of small businesses maintained a website; more than half of the remaining 36% planned to have one within a year, however, and they were being inspired to do so by current technical applications, which offer simpler, more affordable ways of building websites. You need a website to show you are real and to offer information about your business. Think of your website as a home base for your other marketing efforts. For nominal creation and hosting costs, you can have a professional website that conveys much more about your business than the products you sell. A well-designed website has these fundamentals:

- *Tells Who and What:* Visitors recognize immediately your company's basics: who you are and what you sell. Don't leave them guessing for long because web users today have short attention spans. Give them the information they're searching for before they move on to find it more easily at a competitor's site.
- *Reinforces Your Brand:* Your website design, images, and text convey your company's personality, purpose, ethics, policies, and more. Creating your site's pages and contents requires you to clarify your business strengths and all you have to offer.
- *Is Search Engine Optimized:* Search engine optimization ensures that your website can be found in search engines for words and phrases relevant to what your company offers. It is as much art as it is science, but at its core is the discipline of making user-friendly and useful content understandable and easily digestible for search engines.
- *Has Mobile-Friendly Design:* Mobile-friendly design means your website's information—images, texts, videos, and links—is readily accessible across all different platforms and, most particularly, on the much smaller screens of smartphones and tablets. At a more complex level, mobile-friendly design means leveraging all the powerful capabilities of mobile devices to deliver an effective, satisfying experience to users on the go.
- *Is Responsive:* Consumers today will wait about 3 seconds for your site to load before moving on to

another. If you're going past 3 seconds, streamline your home page, simplify the code, or upgrade servers.

- *Incorporates Things That Keep Visitors Coming Back:* Educating visitors is a good start. Getting them to return again and again is the challenge. One technique is to make free features available only to registered users. (That list of names becomes a handy marketing tool, too.) Dr. Siegal's cookiediet.com makes its weight-loss calculators, recipes, meal guidelines, and customizable goal sheets available only to those who register. Those free and meaningful features require continual updates from customers that keep them coming back.
- *Tells Your Brand Story:* Many corporate websites that have been in operation for many years have a History tab under the About Us section. Typically, it includes a timeline that starts on the founding day and shows facts, photos, and a chronology of product introductions, expansions, and other events. The most interesting websites, though, go beyond the timeline to tell stories that reveal the soul of the company. Such foundational stories allow current leaders to draw on the past to highlight themes critical to today's customers and employees.
- *Encourages Interaction:* Provide ways for your website visitors to easily reach out to you. Consider providing an interactive chat feature. Make sure your company's contact information (e.g., email address, phone number, mailing address, link to a Google map) is current and conspicuous throughout the site.

The Brass Lantern Inn site (https://brasslanternnantucket.com/) is impressive on desktop and mobile. The layout is easy to navigate and is filled with photos and videos to show you around the property. It has a user-friendly reservations system and integrated features like a weather app, maps, and gift certificate purchasing. Visitors have an easy user experience, making them more likely to complete a booking on the website.The GSK website (https://www.gsk.com/) has intuitive links to its regional sites and contact pages, use of the website to promote its responsible activities, and simple navigation.

SOCIAL MEDIA

Your customers are already interacting with brands through social media, and if you're not speaking directly to your audience through social platforms such as Facebook, Twitter, Instagram, and Pinterest, you're missing out. Social media marketing can help you:

- Increase website traffic.
- Build conversions with existing and prospective customers.
- Raise brand awareness.
- Create a brand identity and positive brand association; and
- Improve communication and interaction with key audiences.

Social media marketing is crucial and involves creating and sharing content on social media networks to achieve your marketing and branding goals. It includes activities such as posting text and image updates, videos, and other content that drives audience engagement, as well as paid social media advertising.

BUSINESS NETWORKING

Business networking involves leveraging your business and personal connections to bring you a regular supply of new business. It helps you form mutually beneficial business relationships. You must be proactive when networking. Not everyone you meet can help move your business forward, but everything you do can be driven by the intention to grow your business. You have total control over who you meet, where you meet them, and how you develop and leverage relationships for mutual benefit. There are several types of business networking groups (examples below), and what works best for you depends on the business you are in and the prospects you want to meet.

- *Casual contact networks:* These are general business groups that include many people from various overlapping professions. These groups usually meet monthly and often hold mixers where everyone mingles informally. The best examples of these groups are the thousands of chambers of commerce. They offer participants an opportunity to make valuable contacts with many other businesspeople in the community. By attending chamber events, you can make initial contacts that will be valuable in other aspects of developing your referral business.
- *Strong contact networks:* Organizations whose purpose is mainly to help members exchange business referrals are known as strong contact referral groups. Some of these groups meet weekly, typically over lunch or breakfast. Most of them limit membership to one member per profession or specialty. You won't meet hundreds of businesspeople in this type of group, but all the members will be carrying your business cards around with them wherever they go.

- *Community service clubs:* Unlike more business-oriented groups, service groups aren't set up primarily for referral networking; their activities are focused on service to the community. However, through the giving of time and effort to civic causes, you form lasting relationships that broaden and deepen your personal and business networks.
- *Professional associations:* Professional association members tend to be from one specific type of industry, such as banking, architecture, personnel, accounting, or health. The primary purpose of a professional association is to exchange information and ideas.
- *Online or social media networks:* From a business perspective, the ideal use for social media is to build your brand and your credibility with the people you're connected to by providing value for your connections and followers. Whether you're talking about face-to-face networking or online networking, credibility and relationship building are still critical to the process.

ADVERTISING

Advertising is the paid form of your company's message communicated through various media. It is persuasive and informational and is designed to influence the purchasing behavior and/or thought patterns of your audience. Successful advertising spreads the word about your company, attracts customers, and generates sales. Whether you are trying to encourage new customers to buy an existing product or launching a new one, there are many options from which to choose:

- *Newspaper:* Newspaper advertising can promote your business to a wide range of customers. Display advertisements are placed throughout the paper, and classified listings are under subject headings in a specific section. You may find that a combination of advertising in your state or metropolitan newspaper and your local paper gives you the best results.
- *Magazine:* Advertising in a specialist magazine can reach your target market quickly and easily. Readers (your potential customers) tend to read magazines at their leisure and keep them for a while, giving your advertisement multiple chances to attract attention. Magazines generally serve consumers (by interest groups, e.g., women) and trades (by industry, e.g., hospitality). Magazines do not usually serve a small area such as a specific town. If your target market is only a small percentage of the circulation, magazine advertising may not be cost effective.
- *Radio:* If your target market listens to a radio station, then regular advertising on it can attract new customers. Radio advertising has its limitations, however. Listeners can find it difficult to remember what they have heard, and sometimes its impact is lost. The best way to overcome this is to repeat your message regularly, which will also increase your costs.
- *Television:* Television has an extensive reach, which is ideal if you cater to a large market in a large area.

Television advertisements are particularly useful if you need to demonstrate how your product works. Producing a television advertisement and then buying an advertising slot is generally expensive. Advertising is sold in units (e.g., 20, 30, or 60 seconds), and costs vary according to the time slot, the television program being broadcast, and whether the program is seen in a metropolitan or regional area. Also, keep in mind the video power of television advertising on social media and streaming platforms.

- *Directories:* Directories list businesses by name or category (e.g., online directories). Customers who refer to directories have often already made up their mind to buy; they just need to decide from *whom* they will buy. If your target market uses print and online directories, it may be useful to advertise in both, although print directories are being used less and less. The major advantage of online directories over print directories is that if you change your business name, address, or telephone number, you can easily keep it up to date in the directory. You can also add new services or information about your business.
- *Outdoor and transit signs:* There are many ways to advertise outside and on the go. Outdoor billboards can be signs by the road or at sports stadiums. Transit advertising can be posters on buses, taxis, and bicycles. Large billboards can get your message across with a big impact. If customers pass your billboard daily on their way to work, yours is likely to be the first business they think of when they want to buy the product you sell.

- *Direct mail:* Direct mail involves writing to customers directly. The more precise your mailing list or distribution area, the more of your target market you will reach. A direct mail approach is more personal because you can select your audience and plan the timing to suit your business. A cost-effective form of direct mail is to send newsletters or flyers electronically to an email database. Including a brochure with your direct mail communications is a great way to give an interested customer more information about your products.

PUBLIC RELATIONS

Public relations is the field in which coverage for clients is created for free rather than by marketing or advertising. The aim of public relations is to inform the public, prospective customers, investors, partners, employees, and other stakeholders and ultimately persuade them to maintain a positive or favorable view of your company. An example of good public relations would be your publishing an article featuring a client rather than paying for an advertisement in which the client appeared.

EVENTS

Event marketing involves face-to-face contact between companies and your customers at special events such as concerts, fairs, and sporting events. In contrast to traditional advertising, which sends the same general television, radio, or billboard message to many consumers, event marketing targets specific individuals or groups at gathering spots, in hopes of making quality individual impressions. Successful events provide value to attendees beyond information about your company. A discount, free sample, charity alignment, or fun event will make customers feel as though they are receiving a benefit and not just attending a live-action commercial. The key to sponsoring an effective event-marketing campaign is to identify the target audience correctly and create an experience that remains in participants' memories. By finding an opportunity to interact with the right demographic of people—both current customers and prospective buyers—a brand can build favorable impressions and long-lasting relationships. The best, most creative events prompt interactions that not only reflect positively on the brand at the time but generate a buzz long after the event is over.

Cosmetics Company Event

For example, a cosmetic company sponsored an event where they featured a television celebrity's personal makeup artist. He presented three hours on how he makes African American women look twenty years younger than they are. Hundreds of women attended and paid to do so. The company gave a cosmetic bag to all attendees free of charge.

TRADE SHOWS

Trade shows are exhibitions at which businesses in a particular industry promote their products. People attend trade shows to find out what's new and unique in the business. Trade shows are sponsored by trade associations for specific industries, and there are thousands of associations running shows every year. Generally, trade shows aren't open to the public and can only be attended by company representatives and members of the press. Exhibiting at a trade show is an excellent way to find customers to help your business grow. According to a study conducted by the Center for Exhibition Industry Research, 86% of show attendees were decision makers or persons who influenced buying decisions, yet 85% had not been called on by a salesperson before the show. Trade shows are also economical ways of getting sales. Closing a sale that begins with contact at a trade show runs about half the cost of closing a sale that doesn't have the exhibition advantage: If you can figure out where your customers are, you should be there.

INFLUENCERS

A marketing rule of thumb is that in any given market, 1% are influencers, 9% are promoters, and the remaining 90% constitute the market. As social networks continue to evolve and users increasingly rely on more accessible, immediate, word-of-mouth recommendations, a growing number of businesses are turning to influencer marketing to maximize the reach of their messaging. In marketing terms, influencers are persons (usually), groups, brands, or places that can make creditable claims about a product that might cause others to buy it. Celebrities or bloggers may, for example, be influencers. Total brand spending on influencer marketing was $81 billion in 2016 and is projected to reach $101 billion by 2020, according to a 2017 study from the Association of National Advertisers and PQ Media.

Studies show that 93% of people will try things recommended by friends. The closest most businesses will get to having a "friend" recommend their product is having an influencer, or someone that consumers might turn to for relevant, trusted advice, make a recommendation.

Cosmetics Company Influencer

For example, the owner of a cosmetics company (a consumer business) found his best influencers to be video bloggers, in this case, women who applied fine makeup. He was amazed at how many women spent time online watching other women put on makeup and how many then bought the products. As a result, he invited eight influential newspaper editors to visit his company in Japan and served as their host while they were in his country. The entire time there, the visitors were Instagramming, Facebooking, and writing articles about why they loved his cosmetics line. The editors became influencers, just as the video bloggers had.

Influencers need not be famous or have millions of followers; they need only have enough sway and enough of a following to influence your target audience. The benefit of being able to reach users in this way can be significant.

In some industries, influencers have a different or lesser effect than in the cosmetics industry or they may be significant at different points in the sales cycle. This would be the case for influencers of business-to-business (B2B) sales. Reaching B2B decision makers isn't as easy as reaching consumers. An influencer with a large following on Snapchat or Instagram doesn't have much credibility with B2B buyers, unless the influencer happens to work in IT, which isn't a typical scenario. Also, B2B buyers don't typically click on a link from an Instagram post, go to a corporate website, and purchase software. They usually start the purchase process by reading reviews, studying technical specifications, and Googling for information. This behavior is usually the result of a conversation they had with a peer or coworker. They spend hours, days, and sometimes months researching the technology, asking questions, and bouncing ideas off their network. The minimum average sales cycle for enterprise software is 6 months. Although social media has accelerated this cycle, it's still much longer than the cycle for consumer products. It's said that B2B buyers get as far as two thirds of the way through the purchase journey before they contact a vendor, and that's only if the vendor's capability meets their basic technical requirements. B2B buyers are sophisticated, well educated, and skeptical about sales and marketing. For them, trusted third parties are the best influencers.

Influencers and analysts can at times be difficult to work with. For instance, an analyst might produce a negative review of your company's product, saying that it is a niche solution that works only for financial services. The positive side of this is that a financial services company might see this review and realize that you have the perfect solution for the firm's need. In this way, even bad press can be better than no press.

STRATEGIC PARTNERSHIP

A strategic partnership is a relationship between two companies, usually formalized by a contract. Typically, the companies form this partnership when each possesses one or more business assets or has expertise that will help the other enhance its business. A common strategic partnership involves one company that can provide engineering, manufacturing, or product development services to a smaller firm or an inventor who is creating a specialized new product. Typically, the larger firm supplies capital and the necessary capabilities, and the smaller firm supplies specialized technical or creative expertise. Another common strategic partnership involves a supplier or manufacturer partnering with a distributor or wholesale consumer.

Strategic Partnership Examples

As examples, an automotive manufacturer may form strategic partnerships with its parts suppliers, or a music distributor with record labels. Strategic partnerships also have emerged to solve company business problems. Firms taking advantage of strategic partnerships can utilize other company's strengths to make both firms stronger in the long run.

RETURN ON INVESTMENT: IS YOUR MARKETING EFFECTIVE?

Your marketing may be entertaining, but is it effective? The bottom line is that it must stimulate sales. A cosmetics company offered a weekend promotion at a department store where they gave a free cosmetics bag to each customer who purchased its product. Each bag cost the company a dollar; they gave away one hundred bags and earned one thousand dollars above what they normally would have made during the same period without the promotion. It is relatively easy to calculate their return on that marketing investment.

There are many formulas and much advice offered in the area of determining your marketing effectiveness and return on investment. Because most of your marketing efforts should drive prospective customers to your website, one good way to begin is by gathering data related to its use, including

- *Unique visitors:* The best indication of your site's overall traffic, this number indicates how many individuals visit your website during a given time; each visitor is only counted once. This number will vary dramatically depending on the size of your company, your industry, and the amount of content you're producing.
- *Page views:* This is the cumulative number of individual pages that your visitors click on during a given period. If your page views are more numerous than your unique

visitors, it may be an indication that your audience is finding your content engaging because individuals are clicking around to multiple pages.

- *Search engine traffic:* This is the amount of traffic being referred to your site through search engines, such as Google or Bing. This number will give you a clear indication of how effective a job you are doing at optimizing your content for searching.
- *Bounce rate:* This rate is the percentage of visitors who come to your site and then immediately "bounce," or leave, before clicking on any of your other pages. A bounce rate of less than 40% is considered good. If it is any higher, it may be an indication that visitors to your site don't like what they find there.
- *Conversion rate:* This is the percentage of visitors to your site who take a specific action that your content encourages them to take, such as signing up for your newsletter. Conversion rates vary considerably based on industry; they tend to hover around 2% or 3% on average. Aim for a conversion rate of approximately 5% or even higher if you are creating specific landing pages for specific audiences.
- *Inbound links:* The number of external links to your site is an indication that other people have found your content important enough to link to it. Importantly, the more high-quality inbound links you have, the higher your content will rank on search engines.

One of the best ways to track all this information is by setting up a free account with Google Analytics. A powerful tool, Google Analytics allows you to monitor your website and analyze a large amount of data at both the aggregated and individual page level. That way you can find out how specific pieces of content are performing, as well as the overall performance of your content marketing efforts. Signing up is easy and takes just a few minutes. Within a matter of days, Google Analytics will have collected enough data to allow you to start analyzing trends and looking for new insights.

THE PIECES FALL INTO PLACE

"If you can't summarize an issue on one page, you don't understand the issue well enough"

Ronald Reagan

One of the most difficult things about the marketing quadrant is that there are so many options from which to choose. Creating your plan helps you document your decisions on what you will market, as well as how, when, and to whom. It helps remind you to be clear about your brand and story and make sure you know your customer, your competition, and what differentiates you from the competition. Don't spend money on your marketing until you are clear on these things. Also, keep in mind there is no marketing silver bullet or a one-size-fits-all marketing plan. Every business is different; the marketing plan and tactics for a mortgage broker are entirely different from those of a computer reseller. An e-commerce or travel business, being highly visual, can get significant value from a strong presence on Instagram or Pinterest. A B2B or marketing company might find more leverage in Twitter or LinkedIn. Whatever your business, focus on consistent messages and replay them often. Many marketing professionals believe in the "rule of seven," which means people need to hear or see your message at least seven times before they will take any action on it.

CHAPTER 7

STAY THE COURSE

"Some people dream of success, while other people get up every morning and make it happen."
Wayne Huizenga

There you have it, the wisdom gleaned from our combined 60 years of helping business owners manage and grow their companies captured in a four-quadrant Concentric Growth Model. Now that you've been introduced to the model in Chapter 1, taken your self-assessments in Chapter 2, and read more about each of the four quadrants in Chapters 3 through 6, you should have at this point identified areas in which you need to do better and possibly determined which talents you need to bring on board.

When you step back from the details, keep in mind that the most important goals are to (1) get your product in front of customers and (2) get the customers' continuous, honest feedback on it. A catchy marketing campaign combined with the best sales team in the world can't sell products that customers don't want or need. All four quadrants—product, sales, customer, marketing—are important, but the most critical one is the customer quadrant. When customers are willing to buy from you (again and again) and recommend you to others, it gives you confidence that your company is on the right track.

Having worked with business owners for many years, we understand the stress they endure and the ups and downs they go through. Not every business deal gets closed, not every quarter delivers the hoped-for financial results, and not every customer agrees to be a reference. You're going to have uplifting days where you think, "I'm on the right path and this is great!" and you're going to have stretches where you say, "What in the world am I doing? How can I afford to pay the monthly bills and my daughter's college tuition and handle all life's pressures? Why don't I just go look for a job?" During those times, *take a deep breath* and accept that you'll go through periods where you will question what you are doing. During the tough times, you need to find solace in areas that are doing well and make plans to address things that aren't. Keep reminding yourself of what your mission is, where you're going, where you are, and why what you are doing is so important to you. You need to compartmentalize, too, and do your best to separate your business life from your personal life.

Finances are critical. Each of the four quadrants needs funding, whether it be for initial product development or subsequent enhancements, to hire top-shelf salespeople, for attending trade shows where you can be in contact with your target customers, or to deploy marketing campaigns. Because there's so much information available about obtaining venture capital and raising finances, we chose not to cover those topics in our book. Put together an elevator pitch, a brief, persuasive speech that you can use potential investors to spark interest in what your company does. A good elevator pitch should last no longer than a short elevator ride of 20 to 30 seconds; hence, the name.

> ## Airbnb
>
> Don't be discouraged if you have trouble finding investors. Airbnb is a privately held global company headquartered in San Francisco that operates an online marketplace and hospitality service. Members can use the service to arrange or offer lodging, primarily homestays, or tourism experiences. Against all odds, with no prospective investors in sight and thousands of dollars of credit card debt accumulated, the founders kept going; they had to resort to selling breakfast cereals to keep the company afloat. It took almost 2 years from its start in 2007 before Airbnb gained some traction. Today, it's a $25-billion-dollar company. It's a good example of a great idea that didn't immediately catch the attention of investors, including noted venture capitalist Fred Wilson, who said "No thanks."

We suggest that quarterly—or twice a year at a minimum—you re-read Chapter 2 and answer the self-assessment questions to provide you with a snapshot of where you are doing well and where you need work in the product, sales, customer, and marketing quadrants. Put written goals in place that, when accomplished, will help you grow steadily. The goals need not be lengthy or complicated; you can simply make a list of to-dos for each quadrant that will help you keep all four quadrants in mind and growing in synch.

If you've ever played golf, you know what a difficult, frustrating, yet exhilarating game it can be. After a string of bogeys, double bogeys, and other bad shots, you're ready to quit the game. Then you come to a hole where you crush a perfect drive, land a crisp shot onto the green in regulation, and sink a lengthy birdie putt. "I love this game!" you think. Running your business is that way. It's hard work. Some days are bogey days; some days are worse. But when you sink a birdie, you realize how rewarding and fun things can be. The main message we want you to take from our book is this: Keep believing in yourself, stay the course, and as we said at the beginning, all the best to you on your journey!

Appendix

This appendix contains blank forms you can use to record a self-assessment of your company's product, sales, customer, and marketing quadrants. You can also go to our webpage and obtain a free assessment. (http://www.tgigc.io/). Use the following as your guide:

- 1. You have given this a lot of thought and you have executed
- 2. You are aware and you have started to work on this
- 3. You need to give this more time.

PRODUCT SELF-ASSESSMENT

Questions	1	2	3
How well do you understand what product(s) you sell, to whom you sell them, and why your customers buy them?			
How relevant is your product in today's market?			
How well do you understand your competition?			
In a crowded marketplace, how well do you understand your key differentiators?			
How able are you to adjust your product to meet changing customer needs?			
Are adequate quality control processes in place?			
Do you have the right people with the right skills in place to deliver your product?			
How confident are you that you have legal, approved-by-regulators, protection for your product or idea?			
How well is your business prepared to handle growth?			
How strong is your inventory and scalability to meet customer demand?			
How complete and current is your plan for the evolution of your product and your company?			
How is your product priced in the market for your growth and profitability?			

SALES SELF-ASSESSMENT

Questions	1	2	3
How effective is your sales team recruitment process?			
How well-defined are your interview and onboarding processes and how closely do you adhere to them?			
Do you have an effective training process and materials in place?			
How good are you at retaining your top salespeople?			
Do you have a margin in place, that is, a must-have minimum to achieve on every deal?			
Do you have financial incentives in place for performance?			
Do you clearly know what makes your product stand out?			
How well-defined, understood, and followed is your account planning process?			
How well-defined and followed is your sales cycle?			
How much knowledge do you have about the most effective way to sell your products?			
How well do your sales teams close sales?			
How well do you manage your sales pipeline?			
How well-defined is your supply chain, from sourcing through distribution?			
How skillful are you at identifying reference customers who can help your sales?			

CUSTOMER SELF-ASSESSMENT

Questions	1	2	3
How good are you at knowing who your customers are?			
How extensive is your knowledge of what your customers think of your product?			
How well do you understand what you want your customer experience to be?			
If your customers differ by channel or type, do you have a strategy for each?			
How would you rate your customer service?			
How aware are you of what customer needs are not being met by your company?			
Do you understand your cost structure for products so that you can produce the best products at the most advantageous prices?			
Do you have a product pipeline?			
How aware are you of the cycle time for your products?			
How well does your cycle time accommodate scaling up?			
How aware are you of how your customers would rate their satisfaction with your company?			
Is your product delivery customer friendly?			
How aware are you of whether your customer wants to hear from you and at what frequency?			
How adept are you at sharing and applying customer feedback to improve your company?			

MARKETING SELF-ASSESSMENT

Questions	1	2	3
How well do you understand your brand?			
How unique is your brand?			
How well does your brand represent your entire family of products?			
How clearly are you conveying your brand in your current marketing efforts?			
How accommodating are you about solving problems for a customer?			
How well do you know your company's story?			
How clearly are you communicating that story in your current marketing efforts?			
How clear are you about which customers or businesses are the focus of your marketing strategies?			
Do you have developed personas about the customer base that can help guide your marketing?			
How integrated is your marketing with other parts of your company (e.g., sales, product, finance)?			
How clearly have you defined your marketing audiences by channel?			

Do you know how to reach, market to, and influence your customers?			
How well do you understand (i.e., measure) the effectiveness of your current marketing strategy?			
How would you rate your current marketing plan for such things as completeness and relevance?			
How would you rate your social media effectiveness?			

Recommended Reading

Wall Street Journal bestseller

DONALD MILLER

WITH DR. J.J. PETERSON

MARKETING MADE SIMPLE

A STEP-BY-STEP STORYBRAND GUIDE FOR ANY BUSINESS

ISO 9001:2015
A Complete Guide to Quality Management Systems

ITAY ABUHAV

"Everybody knows marketing is getting too complicated. Allan Dib solves that problem with his brilliant new book. Read it and simplify your life."

THE 1-PAGE MARKETING PLAN

GET NEW CUSTOMERS, MAKE MORE MONEY, AND STAND OUT FROM THE CROWD

ALLAN DIB

Acknowledgements

Bill and David thank Mike Ransom for his patience and experience. Without him, this book would never have gotten finished. Also, Marjorie Toensing for her thorough edits

Bill also thanks:
- His wife and son, Margot & William, for their encouragement
- His sister, Susanne Bierds Gerdes, for her detailed review
- His colleagues and friends at Citibank, IBM, Solace, and BCC Group for many of the ideas that shaped this book.

]

About the Authors

Bill Bierds is a information technology veteran from Citigroup, IBM, Solace, and BCC Group. These companies have provided multiple opportunities for Bill to work at a few start-ups and experience in detail the challenges associated with great ideas and what makes them succeed  or fail. Bill has an MBA from the Fordham University Gabelli School of Business. He lives in Manhattan, where he is active in philanthropic organizations, especially educational organizations that encourage the development of young people and military veterans in disadvantaged communities. In his free time, Bill enjoys yoga, reading, golf, scuba diving, boating, and tennis.

David Dunne been leading business transformations in companies of all sizes. His passion is designing and making change come to life. He has experience helping businesses grow in the four CGM quadrants.  He is a leader in the product space, having helped bring many financial products to market. In the customer space, he managed customer support and implementation of new products and services for multi-billion-dollar deals. In the sales space, David led multiple teams for sales activities in the financial and consumer goods/retail industries. In the marketing space, he has managed mega-corporate transformation, consumer goods marketing, and PR efforts. David is now highly engaged as an investor and board member by the opportunities presented in venture capital work. David enjoys watching his sons' swimming events, playing golf, scuba diving, writing, travel, and attending tennis events with his wife.

Michael Ransom is a professional writer who specializes in biographies, company histories, and personal profiles. He lives in Rochester, Minnesota, with his wife, Jeanine. Over the past 20 years, he has written more than 20 biographies,  *Mom, Dad, ... Can We Talk?* (a book for baby boomers to help them help their parents navigate their later years), Rochester Minnesota Golf and Country Club's history *(Celebrating a Century),* the Rochester Charter House Retirement Community history *(Our Roots and Our Spirit),* and numerous articles for magazines. In addition to writing, Mike enjoys reading, music, movies, coffee shops, bookstores, jogging, and spending time with his family.

"Who am I? That's the real question, isn't it? Who-who am I? Who are you! What other questions are there? What other questions are there, really! You want to understand the universe? Embrace the universe. The door to the universe is you."

Tom Hanks
"Joe"
Joe Versus the Volcano
1990 Amblin Entertainment

www.ingramcontent.com/pod-product-compliance
Lightning Source LLC
Chambersburg PA
CBHW060848220526
45466CB00003B/1280